COLLECT
MOMENTS
NOT THINGS

COLLECT MOMENTS, NOT THINGS

An Hachette UK Company
www.hachette.co.uk

Summersdale Publishers Ltd
Part of Octopus Publishing Group Limited
Carmelite House
50 Victoria Embankment
LONDON
EC4Y 0DZ
UK

www.summersdale.com

Printed and bound in China

ISBN: 978-1-78783-240-4

Substantial discounts on bulk quantities of Summersdale books are available to corporations, professional associations and other organizations. For details contact general enquiries: telephone: +44 (0) 1243 771107 or email: enquiries@summersdale.com.

COLLECT
MOMENTS

➤

NOT THINGS

Ideas and Inspiration
for Creating a Life
to Remember

TAMSIN KING

summersdale

CONTENTS

THE SMALL HAPPY MOMENTS ADD UP. A LITTLE BIT OF JOY GOES A LONG WAY.

Melissa McCarthy

INTRODUCTION

Walk a llama. Fly a kite. Go stargazing. Ride a steam train. Row a boat. Watch a waterfall. Wonder at life and all its beautiful moments because you only get one chance at it. Seize every opportunity to immerse yourself in nature or do something that involves an experience rather than a commodity. Stop worrying about not having the latest smartphone or laptop. Stop wasting your money on more and more items of clothing that will lie dormant in your wardrobe. Use that money to make memories instead.

Use this book to make that change.

From small, precious, fleeting moments to bigger, one-off, more extravagant experiences, *Collect Moments, Not Things* offers a wealth of ideas to help spark your wanderlust, inspire many new adventures and, most importantly, help you to spend that little extra time away from the digital world. Enjoy!

WHILE YOU ARE ALIVE,
COLLECT MOMENTS NOT THINGS,
EARN RESPECT NOT MONEY AND
ENJOY LOVE NOT LUXURIES.

Aarti Khurana

Collecting Moments on a Small Budget

You don't need lots of money to live a happy life. In fact, most of the ideas in this section are activities you can do for free or at a small cost. You can enjoy them on your own, with your family or friends, or as a large group. Notice that some of the idea pages are followed by note pages, where you can jot down your experiences, and at the back of the book is a month-by-month journal where you can record the activities you enjoyed throughout the year and how they made you feel. Filling in these sections will make you realize how wonderful it is to collect moments, not things.

CLIMB A HILL OR MOUNTAIN... AND VIEW THE WORLD FROM A DIFFERENT PERSPECTIVE

Research a high point close to where you live, don your walking boots and don't forget the walking poles. Walking is a fantastic way to practise mindfulness: let the rhythmic pattern of placing one foot in front of the other relax you and allow you to focus on being at one with the activity and nature. Feel the ground beneath your feet and think more deeply about how you are connected to the earth.

The journey alone should make you feel at peace with yourself and your surroundings, but the best part for most will be reaching the destination. Make sure you give yourself enough time to take a rest at the peak and admire the

panoramic views. You could even prepare a picnic to take with you to enjoy after all that walking.

As you sit there, take note of the weather: is your body being warmed by the heat of the sun? Is the constant breeze waking up your body and asking you to acknowledge how it feels? Before you begin the climb down, go to each compass point at the top and see how the landscape changes. Capture a snapshot of each view to store in your memory, taking in the small details as well as the bigger picture. Before you even reach ground level, you'll have made the decision to go on another climbing adventure.

A VIEW TO REMEMBER

After spending the day in the great outdoors,
jot down some details about the experience so
that the memory will never lose its clarity.

DATE:
....

LOCATION:
....

WEATHER:
....

....

WILDLIFE YOU SAW ALONG THE WAY:
....

....

FLORA YOU SAW ALONG THE WAY:
....

....

WHAT YOU SAW FROM YOUR BIRD'S-EYE VIEW:
....

....

....

DATE:

LOCATION:

WEATHER:

WILDLIFE YOU SAW ALONG THE WAY:

FLORA YOU SAW ALONG THE WAY:

WHAT YOU SAW FROM YOUR BIRD'S-EYE VIEW:

FIND A SPOT WITHOUT ANY LIGHT

POLLUTION ON A CLEAR NIGHT

Take a rug or mat with you and lie down, looking up at the stars. Switch off your phone so you have no distractions and enjoy the peaceful surroundings. To help you focus on certain areas of the sky, you might want to take some binoculars or a telescope, or even just a paper tube (it works!), with you. Appreciate the cosmos that is spread out in front of you. Take a moment to wonder at the vastness of the skies and how you are a part of this scene – it helps you to put everything into perspective.

STARRY-EYED OBSERVATIONS

As you wonder at the jewel-encrusted night sky and let everything else disappear from your mind, try jotting down some details on what you saw and how the experience made you feel. Turn back to these pages when you are having a down day and remember the serenity of the moment. You will want to relive it all over again!

DATE: .... TIME: ....

LOCATION: .... DURATION: ....

OBSERVATIONAL METHODS

☐ NAKED EYE ☐ PAPER TUBE

☐ BINOCULARS ☐ TELESCOPE

CONSTELLATIONS I SAW
(*DRAW OR WRITE DOWN WHAT YOU SAW*)

HOW THE MOMENT FELT ....
....

DATE: ....

TIME: ....

LOCATION: ....

DURATION: ....

OBSERVATIONAL METHODS

☐ NAKED EYE   ☐ PAPER TUBE

☐ BINOCULARS   ☐ TELESCOPE

CONSTELLATIONS I SAW
(*DRAW OR WRITE DOWN WHAT YOU SAW*)

HOW THE MOMENT FELT ....

....

THERE WAS NOWHERE TO GO BUT EVERYWHERE, SO JUST KEEP ON ROLLING UNDER THE STARS.

Jack Kerouac

REASONS TO COLLECT MOMENTS,
Not Things

#1: *Moments last longer*

Yes, you could splash out on a treat, such as some clothes or a gadget, but after a while the novelty of this shiny brand-new thing will have worn off. Instead of constantly multiplying your belongings with things you already have – both wasting money and creating another item to go to landfill – you could be experiencing beautiful moments that you'll remember and cherish forever.

CHAT THE EVENING AWAY

After a long busy day we tend to gravitate toward the sofa and turn on the TV or look at our phones or tablets for the sake of it, even if they don't interest us. Break up this routine by having a no-screen evening at least once a week.

Spend this time with your friends or family and chat the evening away. Don't be afraid of the silences between each conversation, as they will become more natural with time. But if you do find this too daunting, you can always have some games at the ready for when the moment calls. No matter how much you think you know a person, you will always find out new and interesting things about them that you didn't know before.

WHY MOMENTS ARE BETTER THAN THINGS

After focusing your whole self on friends or
family members without the distraction of technology
getting in the way, you may feel pleasantly surprised
by its benefits. Although it's such a simple pastime,
it'll leave you wondering why you've ever let your
phone distract you from the here and now before.

Yet it's very easy to let things slip and get back into
bad habits, so try noting down all the positives you
got from the experience on the following page. Every time
you feel the urge to fill a conversation with
some background noise or leave your phone within
your reachable vicinity (just in case), think
back to these technology-free moments.

POSITIVES OF TECH-FREE MEET-UPS

SET WIDE THE WINDOW.
LET ME DRINK THE DAY.

Edith Wharton

GO OUT IN A DOWNPOUR

Do you check your weather app for a 24-hour update on wind speeds, daylight hours and the likelihood of precipitation in order to time your day around any bad weather? Well, try ditching those habits and get ready for a stroll in a downpour.

Of course, it's best to be sensible and gear up in your waterproofs, a hooded water-resistant coat and some sturdy boots or wellingtons so that you don't catch a chill, but other than that it's time to throw caution to the wind. Splash your way through puddles and feel the incessant pattering of water droplets on your face. There's something incredibly liberating about being out in the rain, especially when the streets are empty as everyone else tries to keep dry indoors.

GO FOR A CLEAN-UP WALK

Who would have thought picking up litter off the ground would make you feel so good? Whenever you go out for a walk, take a bin bag with you and pick up the plastic bottles, food wrappers and discarded household items you see on your way. Wear some gloves if you don't feel comfortable collecting it with your bare hands.

Although this activity isn't the most glamorous, you'll be surprised at how good you feel afterwards, knowing that you've done something good for the planet.

GO DOG WALKING

Studies show that the average dog owner walks approximately 9 hours per week! Further studies have linked dog walking to happiness and many other health benefits. What's more, you get to spend time with a bundle of fluffy joy – it's a win–win! Even if you don't have a dog there are ways to take a dog for a walk. Online sites allow you to connect with dog owners who need help looking after their dog on a daily or weekly basis – for example, an elderly person who struggles with their mobility – or those who are going on holiday and need someone to look after their dog in their absence.

Whether it's a short walk round the block, a trip to the beach or a stroll in the countryside, you'll feel invigorated with the love you receive from your new tail-wagging, life-loving friend.

TRY STONE SKIMMING

A day at the beach is the perfect cure for any negative vibes you might be harbouring. And you don't always have to go when it's sunny. In fact, the best times are usually when the weather is a little overcast or in the winter as there's more of the beach to enjoy on your own, without the sunbathers getting in the way.

To master the art of stone skimming, you should make sure you visit the beach on a day when the sea is calm and there aren't many people around. You can also practise skimming stones on a river or lake, but pebbly coastlines are best as you have the equipment you need right at your feet.

Find a flat stone, one that is thin and fits nicely in your palm. Hold the stone so that it's resting between your thumb and first finger, with your second finger underneath for support. Once it feels secure in your grip, bring your lower arm and wrist close toward your body and then make a whipping motion with your arm away from your body, releasing the stone as you do so. Aim the throw horizontally so that the stone doesn't fly up in the air. It's best to be as close to the water level as possible for a successful skim. If you're with someone, see who can create the most bounces on the water's surface, and take a moment to watch the ripples expand and disappear. It's quite hypnotic.

GO BUTTERFLY WATCHING

The shapes and colours of butterflies are so varied that once you start actively looking for them, you'll be amazed by how many types there are. They are incredibly beautiful and underrated creatures, and just by focusing on their perfect, graceful stillness when perched on a flower or their hypnotic fluttering movements in the air, you'll feel a sense of calm wash over you.

To find the perfect butterfly-watching spot, go to a location abundant in colourful flowers and long, thick grass. You'll find more of them when it's a sunny and calm day and the temperature is above 20°C (68°F); butterflies like warm and sheltered spots so try visiting an area that's secluded and surrounded by trees and bushes.

The art of butterfly watching is in being patient and attuning your vision to small areas rather than the bigger picture. Be totally focused on the here and now, otherwise a butterfly may escape your wandering eyes. Once you spot one make sure you move slowly and steadily as you get closer to it. If you have them, take some binoculars with you to help you see the butterfly in more detail. Jot down or draw the colours, sizes and shapes of the butterflies you spot on the following pages, and then once you are home you can research which species you found.

BUTTERFLIES I SAW TODAY

DATE: ....

LOCATION: ....

BUTTERFLIES I SAW TODAY

DATE:

LOCATION:

BUTTERFLIES I SAW TODAY

DATE:

LOCATION:

THE PURPOSE OF LIFE IS TO LIVE IT, TO TASTE EXPERIENCE TO THE UTMOST, TO REACH OUT EAGERLY AND WITHOUT FEAR FOR NEWER AND RICHER EXPERIENCE.

Eleanor Roosevelt

FLY A KITE

On a breezy day, get outside and try flying a kite. The perfect condition for this pastime is when it's windy enough to see leaves and bushes moving but not tree branches! Flat, open spaces are great spots to really make the most of this activity, but avoid built-up areas and anywhere close to overhead power lines or big trees that the kite could get tangled up in. Beaches, parks and fields are prime locations to watch your kite soar.

To fly your kite, lay it on the ground, making sure the string isn't tangled up and that your back is to the wind. As you hold the kite's handle, get someone else to hold the kite, so it's pointing upward, and release it when it feels like there's enough wind underneath it to help it take off. To help the kite gain altitude, pull on the line until it reaches a height where there is a strong enough and steady wind.

REASONS TO COLLECT MOMENTS,
Not Things

#2: *Moments teach us valuable lessons*

Every moment you collect is a wonderful way to feel inspired and energized. But even if things don't go entirely to plan, or don't go to plan at all, you'll still have created an experience – one that you'll probably see the funny side of later.

LIFE
is a
tapestry
of
MOMENTS.

WATCH THE SUN RISE OR SET

Imagine starting your day with an early rise and the incredible sight of the sun climbing up over the horizon. Surely nothing could faze you after that? And even if it did, you can use the power of this wonderful sight to eradicate the small anxieties and problems you face. If you aren't an early bird, then there's nothing stopping you from catching the last glimpses of the sun in the evening instead.

No matter what your horizon might be – a faultless seascape, a hilltop vista or even the view from your bedroom window – savour the moments of this most spectacular and natural wonder.

JOIN AN ART OR CRAFT CLUB

You can do this at any time of the year, but it is particularly good in the colder, wetter months. Find a group online, on social media, or create one with your friends and family. You can stick to perfecting one discipline, or you can change what you practise every so often so that you are always expanding your art and crafting skills. Some ideas are:

Calligraphy

Crocheting

Knitting

Sketching

Water-colouring

Quilting

Flower arranging

Soap/candle making

Rubber stamping

Origami

Card making

Decoupage

Scrapbooking

Collaging

EMBRACE WILD SWIMMING

Take a trip to a nearby river, lake or beach – check to make sure it's a place where wild swimming is permitted beforehand – and prepare to take a dip. Depending on where you are and what month it is, you will need to make sure that the swimming gear you take with you is appropriate. If you are going in the middle of winter you'll probably need a wetsuit to keep you warm. Always tell someone of your whereabouts if you intend to go wild swimming on your own.

Go to a water source that your mood is calling for – if you want to feel energized, perhaps a swim in the sea will sort out your needs, or if you want to relax, then a float in a lake may be the ticket. No matter where you go, wild swimming is a fantastic way to feel at one with nature and wash away the stresses of the day.

CAMP OUT IN YOUR GARDEN

Who says you need to camp miles away from home for the ultimate sleeping-under-the-stars experience? If you have a garden, you only have to take one step outside to be in the perfect spot. If you don't have a garden, you could kindly ask someone who does if you can use it for the night.

If you want a wilder experience, choose a night when the weather is unsettled, or if you particularly enjoy staring up at the stars and getting lost in the night sky, then pick a night that's clear and calm.

Just before you drift off to sleep, be perceptive of the surrounding sounds of nature. Living within four walls all the time makes it easy to forget that nature exists. If you do start to feel afraid, be reassured that a place of security is just a few paces away.

IF YOU WANT TO CONQUER
THE ANXIETY OF LIFE,
LIVE IN THE MOMENT,
LIVE IN THE BREATH.

Amit Ray

REASONS TO
COLLECT MOMENTS,
Not Things

 # 3: *Moments strengthen bonds*

By giving technology all of our attention, we run the risk of starving our relationships of the nurture and affection they need to flourish. To put the modern world into perspective, one study found that the average American spends 5 hours on social media every day, while another calculated that Britons check their phones every 12 minutes.

More and more, we have less time for those we love as we continually create unhealthy relationships with our beloved gadgets. But by collecting and sharing more real-life experiences, we can strengthen our ties with friends and family. A moment shared is a moment doubled.

WATCH CLOUDS

It often feels like all we ever do is rush from one job to the next, so to be completely still and watch nature's constant movements is somehow deeply satisfying. The perfect conditions for cloud-spotting are blue skies and a fresh breeze – this will allow the clouds to scud past in continuous and ever-changing formations and help you get the most out of the experience – but the beauty of this activity is that you can do it anytime you happen to be outside.

Look for shapes the clouds make, and dream up stories that follow their movements and changing shapes. Take a moment to feel humbled by the vast expanse of blue that surrounds you. There's no doubt you will feel invigorated for the rest of the day.

MY CLOUD-WATCHING MOMENTS

DATE:
....

TIME:
....

LOCATION:
....

DURATION:
....

TYPE OF CLOUDS
....

....

....

....

WHAT SHAPES I SAW IN THE CLOUDS
....

....

....

....

MY CLOUD STORY
....

....

....

MY MOOD BEFORE
....

....

MY MOOD AFTER
....

....

....

MY CLOUD-WATCHING MOMENTS

DATE:

TIME:

LOCATION:

DURATION:

TYPE OF CLOUDS

WHAT SHAPES I SAW IN THE CLOUDS

MY CLOUD STORY

MY MOOD BEFORE

MY MOOD AFTER

MY CLOUD-WATCHING MOMENTS

DATE: ....

TIME: ....

LOCATION: ....

DURATION: ....

TYPE OF CLOUDS
....

....

....

....

WHAT SHAPES I SAW IN THE CLOUDS
....

....

....

....

MY CLOUD STORY
....

....

....

MY MOOD BEFORE
....

....

MY MOOD AFTER
....

....

....

A FEW SIMPLE TIPS
FOR LIFE: FEET ON
THE GROUND, HEAD
TO THE SKIES, HEART
OPEN... QUIET MIND.

Rasheed Ogunlaru

TRY YOGA OUTSIDE

More and more people are regularly practising yoga to benefit from its numerous physical and mental benefits. It's great anywhere and at any time of day but there is something special about practising it in nature. Find a place where you will be comfortable, whether that's in your garden, at a park or even on a sandy beach, and don't forget your yoga mat. Practising yoga in public may feel daunting at first, but you'll soon forget about the passers-by once you begin.

When performing yoga moves outside, take note of your environment. If it's a warm day, enjoy the sun heating up your muscles and giving you a boosted stretch. If it's cool, start slowly and appreciate how your body warms up as you move through the positions. Feel connected to the ground beneath you and make each pose meaningful by rooting yourself into the earth. As you reach moments of stillness, enjoy the sounds of life continuing around you.

MOMENTS
allow you to
fall in love
with life
AGAIN AND AGAIN.

GO ROCK-POOLING

You may have to travel a little if you live inland,
but rock-pooling is a magical experience
for children and adults alike.

Research the tide times of the beach you wish to visit
and go on a calm day so that the water in the rock
pools is undisturbed. Don't forget your wellies. To get
the most out of the experience, you'll need to get your
hands wet as you turn over rocks to reveal the hidden
creatures beneath them. No matter how excited you
may get, it's best not to touch them; instead, you can be
awed by their beauty from afar. Besides the wonderfully
coloured seaweeds, creatures to look out for are:

Prawns and shrimps

Starfish and brittle stars

Sea hares

Whelks, limpets and mussels

Crabs

Sea anemones

SKETCH YOUR ROCK POOL
FINDINGS HERE

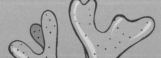

SKETCH YOUR ROCK POOL
FINDINGS HERE

REJOICING IN ORDINARY
THINGS IS NOT
SENTIMENTAL OR TRITE.
IT ACTUALLY TAKES GUTS.

Pema Chödrön

WALK UNDER A WATERFALL

The sound of moving water is free therapy for the soul. Research a nearby waterfall (if you don't live near one, it could be the perfect excuse for a mini excursion) and make travel arrangements, so that you are prepared for the day ahead of time.

If there is a riverside track, enjoy the walk to the waterfall, taking in the natural surroundings. Listen out for the sound of crashing water, a good signal you're heading in the right direction. Once you have reached the waterfall and have taken a few moments to lap up the experience, try closing your eyes. Let the noise of the water shut out any other niggling thoughts inside your mind and allow you to focus completely on the present moment. If there is a safe walkway, stand behind the waterfall for an intense, raw experience as you feel the power of the water free-falling.

If there isn't a waterfall near to where you live or you aren't able to travel to one, opt to go to the beach instead and listen to the musical and calming ebb and flow of water there. It is the perfect way to clear the mind.

DISCOVER FORAGING

Feel at one with the earth and discover foraging, an age-old hunter-gatherer tradition that you can practise all year round. While you embrace the countryside, make the most of nature's cornucopia of offerings, their rainbow colours and heavenly scents. It's advisable to take a little help from a foraging guide to make the most of your experience and to make sure everything you're collecting is edible. Always remember to treat the countryside with respect and appreciate the rewards we reap from it. From berries to herbs and plants to nuts, there is a wide variety of seasonal delights to be found and used in your home cooking. And best of all – it's free!

REASONS TO COLLECT MOMENTS,

Not Things

#4: *Moments give us character*

Experiences build our characters and shape who we are. No matter how big or small the experience is, it is almost guaranteed to help us grow as individuals and form a better understanding of the world we live in. For example, visiting a botanical garden can help you learn more about the natural world and discover new flowers, plants and trees you weren't even aware of before. Or when you next go to a new country, really take note of everything it offers: its culture, history, architecture, transport, food, climate, terrain, animals and people. It's easy to take things for granted, so when you next embark on a new experience, try to savour every second and pay close attention to your feelings, thoughts and observations, as they will help you build on who you are and understand what the world means to you.

WATCH A STARLING MURMURATION

Starlings migrate south for the winter to escape the bitterly cold weather. If you live in Europe or North America, or happen to be visiting in late autumn to early winter, then try to catch a glimpse of this spectacle as it's one of the most dazzling displays put on by nature. Take your camera with you, but make sure you observe this bird ballet with the naked eye too, as it's a moment that all the money in the world can't buy.

ENJOY THE DELIGHTS OF A PYO

If foraging is not your thing, or you're a bit nervous about your ability to identify edible stuff, why not seek out a PYO farm? Seasonally, there are many to choose from and you can enjoy the simplicity of selecting your very own food to eat, safe in the knowledge that you won't be poisoning yourself! The pleasure of eating what you've picked is so much more satisfying than simply buying food from a shop. If you get carried away and come home with an excess of fruit, try your hand at making any extra into preserves.

MOMENTS, RATHER THAN POSSESSIONS, ARE THE TRUE TREASURES OF LIFE.

Frank Sonnenberg

VOLUNTEER FOR A CHARITY CLOSE TO YOUR HEART

Whether it's in a shop, at an animal rescue centre, helping the homeless or going to schools, pick an organization that you want to volunteer for and make it your mission to help out, even if it's just for a few hours per week. Enjoy making a difference to other people's or animals' lives and take note of how good it feels knowing that you have the ability to cheer up another human being or furry friend. It is one of the most selfless activities you can pursue, yet ironically it'll leave you feeling the best you've felt in a long time.

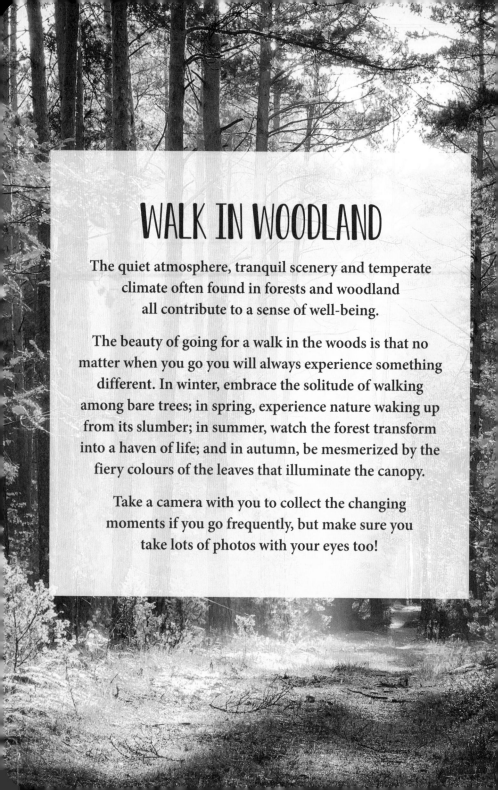

WALK IN WOODLAND

The quiet atmosphere, tranquil scenery and temperate
climate often found in forests and woodland
all contribute to a sense of well-being.

The beauty of going for a walk in the woods is that no
matter when you go you will always experience something
different. In winter, embrace the solitude of walking
among bare trees; in spring, experience nature waking up
from its slumber; in summer, watch the forest transform
into a haven of life; and in autumn, be mesmerized by the
fiery colours of the leaves that illuminate the canopy.

Take a camera with you to collect the changing
moments if you go frequently, but make sure you
take lots of photos with your eyes too!

I FELT ONCE MORE HOW SIMPLE
AND FRUGAL A THING IS HAPPINESS:
A GLASS OF WINE, A ROAST CHESTNUT,
A WRETCHED LITTLE BRAZIER, THE
SOUND OF THE SEA. NOTHING ELSE.

Nikos Kazantzakis

GO BIRD WATCHING

Have you ever had a small bird perch next to you, intrigued by what you are eating, and felt a moment of pure joy at its closeness to you? Bird watching is great for cleansing the soul and bringing calm into your life. More importantly, you can do it anywhere, from your back garden or a local park to an open field.

The only equipment you'll need for bird watching is patience, a decent pair of binoculars and a field guide. Wear dark-coloured clothing, so you blend into your surroundings, and be quiet and still. Take a notebook or this book with you and jot down any sightings, including the time and where you were. If you aren't sure what bird you've seen, write down a description of it or sketch it and use your field guide to discover what it is.

SKETCH OR JOT DOWN
THE BIRDS YOU SAW

SKETCH OR JOT DOWN THE BIRDS YOU SAW

Collecting Moments on a Medium Budget

If you have money left over at the end of the month – now that you aren't buying as many things – you could put it toward some of the ideas in this chapter. You can enjoy them on your own, with your family or friends, or as a large group.

As you bank precious moments, jot down your experiences on the note pages and fill in the month-by-month journal at the back of the book. You only get one chance at life so make it the best it can possibly be by collecting moments, not things!

IT IS THE PREOCCUPATION WITH POSSESSIONS, MORE THAN ANYTHING ELSE, THAT PREVENTS US FROM LIVING FREELY AND NOBLY.

Bertrand Russell

TRY A TREE-TOP TRAIL

Reach new heights as you strap yourself into a harness and climb from tree to tree like a monkey. More and more activities of this nature are springing up all over the place, so you shouldn't have to travel too far to your nearest one. As well as having lots of fun overcoming the obstacles and challenges in your way, make sure you take some moments to study the ancient trees that make this activity possible and feel present in the woodland that surrounds you.

GO CAVING

This activity won't necessarily leave you marvelling at breath-taking views and scenery, but it will heighten your other senses as you climb through small holes and scramble along dark passageways. Only ever do this with an experienced instructor who knows the terrain you are exploring inside out, and always wear the correct gear.

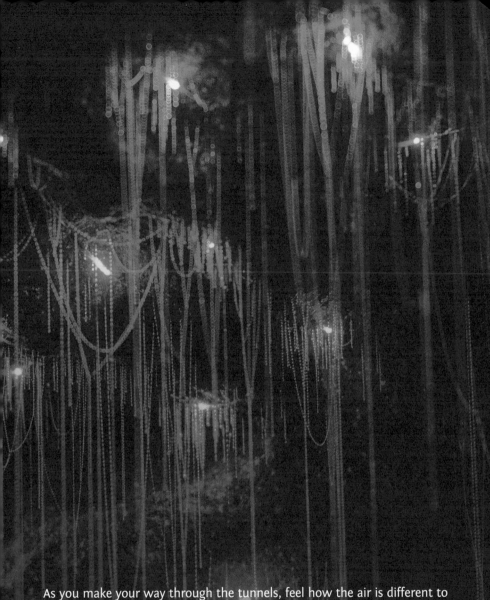

As you make your way through the tunnels, feel how the air is different to above ground and take in the textures and natural materials that sculpt these underground mazes. Sit for a moment without speaking or moving and listen to real silence. If you ever get to a point in the caves that is pitch dark, turn off your head torch and experience the beauty of absolute nothingness. It's a surreal experience, and not in the slightest bit eerie.

BRACE YOURSELF FOR
A COUNTRYSIDE BIKE RIDE

Want to feel alive? Go for a bike ride! Near or far, short or long, flat or hilly, the possibilities are endless! This is a great activity to take part in while on holiday – and if you want to cover a large area of land, such as a national park, try hiring an e-bike, as you'll still feel like you are doing the leg work but it's a lot easier, especially if you are going up and down hills.

Alternatively, nothing beats a weekend cycle close to home, and with so many routes available, you don't have to worry about doing the same one twice. Pack lots of water, sun cream, seasonally appropriate clothing and a bite to eat – or, to make the day even more memorable, look up a restaurant or pub to eat at along the way and make it your destination (a great incentive to cycle with purpose!).

CYCLE SIGHTINGS

As you wind your way along country roads, the landscape around you can become a bit of a blur (especially if you pedal quickly!). So that you're more perceptive to your surroundings, challenge yourself to spot ten interesting sights or landmarks or changes in setting along the way and jot them down on the following pages.

DATE OF BIKE RIDE:
....

LOCATION OF BIKE RIDE:
....

TEN THINGS I SPOTTED ON MY BIKE RIDE

1. ....
....

2. ....
....

3. ....
....

4. ....
....

5. ....

6. ....
....

7. ....
....

8. ....
....

9. ....
....

10. ....

DATE OF BIKE RIDE:

LOCATION OF BIKE RIDE:

TEN THINGS I SPOTTED ON MY BIKE RIDE

1.

2.

3.

4.

5.

6.

7.

8.

9.

10.

CYCLE SIGHTINGS

DATE OF BIKE RIDE:
....

LOCATION OF BIKE RIDE:
....

TEN THINGS I SPOTTED ON MY BIKE RIDE

1. ....
....
....

2. ....
....
....

3. ....
....
....

4. ....
....
....

5. ....
....
....

6. ....
....
....

7. ....
....
....

8. ....
....
....

9. ....
....

10. ....
....

Create
a
SPECIAL MOMENT
and it will
STAY WITH YOU
forever.

ROW, ROW, ROW YOUR BOAT

In the summer months, why waste your time staying indoors when there are so many things to do outside? Why not try your hand at some old-school boating? You can row as slowly or as quickly as you feel like and there's no penalty for stopping and having a break from the exercise. In fact, if you choose to hire a traditional boat with solid wooden oars, you may find that the art of boating is not as easy as it looks!

As you glide along, take the time to be in the present moment. Feel the warmth of the sun on your face and on your body as you bob along on the water's calm surface and enjoy the rhythmic motion of the oars. Observe the wildlife, watching how gracefully ducks move across the water, or how peacefully a dragonfly floats above the surface, and fully embrace the experience, whether you are alone or have company.

REASONS TO COLLECT MOMENTS,
Not Things

5: *Moments are priceless*

It's true that most things cost money. Even if you are visiting somewhere free, chances are you'll have to pay to get there, unless the place is on your doorstep. However, compare the price of these moments with forking out on this season's trainers or another cushion for that already full sofa and you'll be making a massive saving, while creating beautiful memories for the memory bank.

GO SEA KAYAKING
OR PADDLEBOARDING

There's nothing more exhilarating than being in open water, where the sea is your horizon and there's nothing obstructing your view. It's just you and the water around you that exist in that moment in time. Make the most of it.

Depending on what you feel more comfortable doing, either of these two water sports are fantastic for practising mindfulness and strengthening your muscles too. With each stroke, notice the contact you make with the water. Enjoy the fresh sea breeze on your face and the diffusion of salt on your skin as the water splashes you.

There are many coastal hotspots where you can hire kayaks and paddleboards, or if you think you'll use it frequently, why not look into buying your own? Yes, you'll be collecting a thing, but its purpose is to help you experience many wonderful moments.

If you've never practised either sport before, try them out on a lake before you hit the choppy waves. If you're hiring the equipment, it's likely that the shop will offer group or individual lessons for you to gain experience before going out on your own.

THEY HAVE SUCCEEDED IN
ACCUMULATING A GREATER MASS
OF OBJECTS, BUT THE JOY IN
THE WORLD HAS GROWN LESS.

Fyodor Dostoyevsky

LEAD A LLAMA OR TREK WITH AN ALPACA

You may never have heard of it before, but llama and alpaca walking is actually a thing! What could be more fun than wandering along with these wondrous beasts? These organized walks can lift your mood and are guaranteed to put a big smile on your face. While we don't condone taking frequent selfies, a picture with your llama/alpaca guide is a must.

REASONS TO
COLLECT MOMENTS,
Not Things

 # 6: *Moments fill up the diary*

One of the most exciting things about going on holiday is the build-up to it. And this is the same for collecting moments, no matter how big or small. It's lovely to be spontaneous sometimes, but if you're having a stagnant period in your life, plan with friends or family to do something fun and fill that diary up with dates! There's no better feeling than having something to look forward to!

Be mindful of
each moment
AND GRATEFUL
for the
experience.

GO SNORKELLING

It's a misconception that you need to travel to the other side of the world, to gorgeous sandy beaches and crystal-clear seas, to discover the life brimming in our oceans (although it's always a good excuse to go on holiday). So why not explore the beauty of what's just below the surface level of the sea closest to you. If you want guaranteed sightings, check online for the best local places to go snorkelling – organized snorkel trails can be found in many places. Snorkelling equipment can be bought relatively cheaply or it can be hired at water sports kiosks. You may want to think about wearing a wetsuit depending on how cold the water will be and make sure you have a surface marker buoy with you so that you are visible to boats.

DRAW WHAT YOU SAW

WHEN WE GET TOO CAUGHT UP IN THE BUSYNESS OF THE WORLD, WE LOSE CONNECTION WITH ONE ANOTHER - AND OURSELVES.

Jack Kornfield

DANCE LIKE NO ONE IS WATCHING

Dancing is a fantastic way to let off some steam and get lost in the moment. Whether you fancy trying out some tap moves, feeling graceful with ballet or transforming yourself into a sexy salsa dancer, there are classes for all abilities and in all genres for you to choose from. Don't let your embarrassment or nerves get in the way of you experiencing this new activity either. Everyone at the class is doing it because they want to enjoy themselves so leave your insecurities at home and enjoy yourself!

TAKE UP PHOTOGRAPHY

Our lives are overloaded with selfies, where all that's captured is your face. Scrolling back through them, it's difficult to differentiate where and when they were taken. Instead of relentlessly snapping away, capture the magical moments that happen each day in photos that are taken with care and attention, from close-up stills of insects to sprawling cityscapes.

Of course, to take good quality photos, you'll need a good quality camera. And if you've never turned your hand to photography before it would be worth having a lesson or two to help you on your way, especially as there are so many settings to discover on a professional camera.

To start you off with some inspiration of what to shoot, here is a list of objects and scenes that'll spark your creativity:

- **Grass on a dewy morning**
- **Close-ups of garden birds and butterflies**
- **Mushrooms or single flowers**
- **Spider webs**
- **Ladybirds on leaves or flowers**
- **Signs in cities**
- **Parts of a push bike**
- **Architecture**
- **Trains**
- **Sea shells on a beach**
- **Coastlines**
- **Tunnels**
- **Anything nostalgic**
- **Cities at night**
- **Skyscapes**

THE LITTLE THINGS?
THE LITTLE MOMENTS?
THEY AREN'T LITTLE.

Jon Kabat-Zinn

CREATE A COLLAGE
OF YOUR PHOTOS

Refer back to the photos
you took and are proud of
by printing out thumbnails
of them and sticking them
in the following pages.

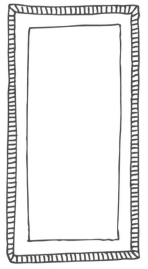

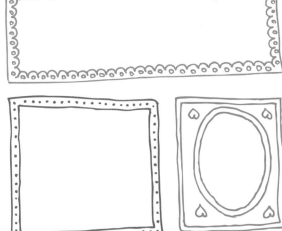

REASONS TO COLLECT MOMENTS,
Not Things

#7: *Moments are more sociable*

It's a common belief that retail therapy is the perfect antidote for a down day. However, recent studies have found that it's the experience of shopping – the social side and exercise – not the buying of products that offers us some relief. The next time you plan to go shopping, why not do all the things you usually do – meeting a friend, catching-up, browsing, going for a bite to eat – but without actually purchasing anything. It'll be just as good and you won't have to lug heavy bags around with you all day!

Collecting Moments on a Bigger Budget

So, you've managed to save up a lump sum of money and want to make sure you spend it on something that you won't forget? Then this chapter is for you.

From diving into the depths of the ocean to floating high in the sky, these are moments that are truly magical and unforgettable.

TAKE A ROAD TRIP IN A CAMPERVAN

Road trips can be as big or as small as you'd like them to be. They can also be done in a basic hire van or in a super-sleek campervan. Whatever tickles your outdoor fancy, make sure you tailor the trip to your tastes. Do you want to be near the sea or the mountains, or in the middle of woodland? Our planet offers so many beautiful spots, both on your doorstep and away from home, that you'll be spoilt for choice.

If it's your first time trying out a camping holiday it might be worth scheduling just a few nights away in case it isn't your scene, but chances are you'll love it! Check out what's going on in the local area and plan some activities that'll get you out and about. And don't forget: a camping holiday is about being as free and mobile as possible, so you can always take detours to other areas of interest along the way. Make the most of collecting beautiful moments while you can!

WANDERING RE-ESTABLISHES THE ORIGINAL HARMONY WHICH ONCE EXISTED BETWEEN MAN AND THE UNIVERSE.

Bruce Chatwin

FLY IN A HOT-AIR BALLOON

Catch the sun rise or set from high in the sky as you float up, up and away. Feel the weight of the world lift off your shoulders as you inch higher and take pleasure in the 360° views as you ascend on your vertical journey. Feel peace and serenity envelop your body as you marvel at the world below you and admire it in all its beauty. This is a moment you'll probably only experience once, but it's one you'll never forget.

REALIZE DEEPLY
THAT THE
PRESENT MOMENT
IS ALL YOU EVER HAVE.

Eckhart Tolle

REASONS TO COLLECT MOMENTS,
Not Things

#8: *Moments are unique to you*

Each moment you collect will be solely yours. Even when you experience something with a group of people, their experiences will always be different to yours, because the way you see, hear, taste and smell things is unique to you.

Unlike the trainers that are in vogue or the handbag that is a must-have because everyone else has it, your experiences are tailor-made and exclusive to you.

TRY CANYONING

If you are a bit of a thrill seeker,
or you just fancy being more
of a daredevil than your day-to-
day life allows, give canyoning
a go. Wade through rivers, climb
up ledges, jump off waterfalls
and swim your way back to land
feeling like an absolute champ.
This is a great organized event for
a group of you and you'll never
forget how much fun you had. But
make sure you always do it with a
qualified guide and never on your
own, as they will know the area
and water levels at different times
of the year. If you want to capture
the experience on video, remember
to take your GoPro with you!

BE PRESENT
in
everything
YOU DO.

LEARN TO SURF

Find a wave and catch it (or try to, anyway). Feel the raw rush of excitement when you stand up on your board and enjoy the water crashing over your body when you fall. It's a great group activity and the perfect way to socialize with fun, active people. There are opportunities to surf all around the world and you can do it in some pretty breath-taking locations. The most revered places to surf, for your surfing bucket list, are:

Hanalei, Hawaii, USA

Byron Bay, Australia

Biarritz, France

Muizenberg, South Africa

Bukit Peninsula, Bali

Santa Cruz, California, USA

Thurso, Scotland

Croyde, England

SAFETY TIP

Never go surfing on your own without an instructor unless you're a confident surfer. The sea is beautiful but dangerous and anything could go wrong if you don't have your wits about you or know what you are doing.

GO TANDEM PARAGLIDING

While on holiday in a mountainous location, view the scenery from a completely different perspective as you glide slowly down to your destination on the ground. Taking off can feel slightly unnerving, but don't let your fears get the better of you as the experience is unparalleled. Once you are in the air, all you have to do is sit back and relax as your experienced glider navigates you safely through the sky. If there was something to make you feel like a bird in flight, this is it.

REASONS TO
COLLECT MOMENTS,
Not Things

#9: *Moments awaken the senses*

Technology has enhanced our lives in many ways, but it has also allowed us to disconnect from the real world we live in and become less confident in making independent decisions. We rely on search engines to give us the answers to all our questions, and as we live linked up to a computer or phone, we become less perceptive of the small, beautiful things happening around us.

For an hour each day, why not have a screen ban and use this time to practise mindfulness? Sit in your back garden or look out of an open window and focus on the noises and things going on around you that you never usually notice. Try closing your eyes and taking a moment to register how you are feeling and how your body feels. You will immediately feel more at peace with yourself and ready to continue the day with vigour.

TAKE A STEAM TRAIN RIDE

Seeing a steam train thunder majestically across the countryside is a rare moment and one some people may only ever experience on the screen. But why not make it your reality instead? Not only will it fill you with nostalgia, you will be able to take in new scenery from the comfort of your plush carriage seat. If you want to make the trip truly memorable, why not treat yourself to afternoon tea or a meal – the view passing the window will be miles better than staring at four walls and a TV while you eat.

Before you board, don't forget to appreciate the train's stately beauty. If you fancy satiating your train fascination, here are some of the best train journeys around the world:

West Highland Line, Glasgow to Mallaig - Scotland

The Ghan - Australia

Trans-Siberian Railway - Russia

Rocky Mountaineer's First Passage to the West - Canada

TranzAlpine - New Zealand

The Flam Railway - Norway

WHAT WOULD IT BE LIKE IF I COULD ACCEPT LIFE – ACCEPT THIS MOMENT – EXACTLY AS IT IS?

Tara Brach

REASONS TO
COLLECT MOMENTS,
Not Things

#10: *Moments make life worth living*

Instead of mindlessly scrolling through your news
feed or reading a dubious article on the latest celebrity
scandal, you could be breathing in the fresh air of forests
or listening to waves forming and breaking. If we all took
a moment to escape from this fake reality we have created
and start discovering the world we have been a part of for
such a long time, we might start to realize there's more to
life than screens.

ENJOY A NARROWBOAT TRIP OR HOLIDAY

It's only when we have a break from our busy lives and do absolutely nothing that we realize how essential it is, both for our bodies and minds. Sometimes it's actually quite difficult to find a place of complete calm without anyone around, but a great way to achieve instant calm is to hire a canal boat. In your vessel you will have guaranteed isolation, apart from when you want to explore, of course, and you'll be left feeling completely rejuvenated as you slowly pass by gorgeous surroundings on calm water. What's more, in most countries where you can hire a canal boat, you don't need a licence to be able to drive it! As long as you take care with manoeuvres and take out ample insurance then the canal and boat is all yours.

On your trip, ensure you make the most of the nature and the views along the way. Try cloud watching (p.46) or bird watching (p.68) while you sit on the terrace of the boat and record your sightings in this book. This trip is also perfect for a romantic getaway if you fancy treating your partner to something a bit different.

The world

is

YOUR OYSTER.

GO HORSE RIDING

Whether you've done it before or you are completely new to it, horse riding will leave you feeling alive. There are horse riding experiences all over the world – you could even make it your goal to go horse riding whenever you travel somewhere new. The instructors will always ensure that you feel safe and secure and, if you need it, they will guide you and the horse every walk, trot and canter of the way. You'll be out in the fresh air, having fun and, what's more, it's a fantastic way to work those muscles and gain good posture.

TRY SCUBA DIVING

Ever wanted to know what it feels like to live underwater? Then arrange for a qualified dive instructor to aid you in taking the plunge into the depths of the deep blue. The sea life you encounter will depend on where your dive takes place, but you're bound to spot something unique on every trip – the underwater world is full of surprises and fascinating creatures wherever you are.

Be dazzled by the feeling of weightlessness and overwhelmed by each breath you take underwater. Attune yourself to the underwater sounds and feel humbled by the endless blue that surrounds you.

A Year of Moments

Make a list of all the moments you want to complete for each month (think about the time of year, what your budget allows and what's available to you). Now write your ideas on the following pages and look forward to filling out the other sections once you've completed the experience.

January

MOMENT ONE

DATE OF MOMENT:

....

....

....

DETAILS OF MOMENT:

....

....

....

HOW IT MADE ME FEEL:

....

....

....

WOULD I DO IT AGAIN?

....

....

MOMENT TWO

DATE OF MOMENT:
....
....
....

DETAILS OF MOMENT:
....
....
....

HOW IT MADE ME FEEL:
....
....
....

WOULD I DO IT AGAIN?
....
....

MOMENT THREE

DATE OF MOMENT:

....

....

....

DETAILS OF MOMENT:

....

....

....

HOW IT MADE ME FEEL:

....

....

....

WOULD I DO IT AGAIN?

....

MOMENT FOUR

DATE OF MOMENT:
....
....
....

DETAILS OF MOMENT:
....
....
....

HOW IT MADE ME FEEL:
....
....
....

WOULD I DO IT AGAIN?
....

MOMENT FIVE

DATE OF MOMENT:
....
....
....

DETAILS OF MOMENT:
....
....
....

HOW IT MADE ME FEEL:
....
....
....

WOULD I DO IT AGAIN?
....
....

MOMENT ONE

DATE OF MOMENT:

....

....

....

DETAILS OF MOMENT:

....

....

....

HOW IT MADE ME FEEL:

....

....

....

WOULD I DO IT AGAIN?

....

....

MOMENT TWO

DATE OF MOMENT:

....

....

DETAILS OF MOMENT:

....

....

HOW IT MADE ME FEEL:

....

....

WOULD I DO IT AGAIN?

....

....

MOMENT THREE

DATE OF MOMENT:
....
....
....

DETAILS OF MOMENT:
....
....
....

HOW IT MADE ME FEEL:
....
....
....

WOULD I DO IT AGAIN?
....
....

MOMENT FOUR

DATE OF MOMENT:

....

....

....

DETAILS OF MOMENT:

....

....

....

HOW IT MADE ME FEEL:

....

....

....

WOULD I DO IT AGAIN?

....

....

MOMENT FIVE

DATE OF MOMENT:
....
....
....

DETAILS OF MOMENT:
....
....
....

HOW IT MADE ME FEEL:
....
....
....

WOULD I DO IT AGAIN?
....
....

March

MOMENT ONE

DATE OF MOMENT:

....

....

....

DETAILS OF MOMENT:

....

....

....

HOW IT MADE ME FEEL:

....

....

....

WOULD I DO IT AGAIN?

....

....

MOMENT TWO

DATE OF MOMENT:

....

....

DETAILS OF MOMENT:

....

....

HOW IT MADE ME FEEL:

....

....

WOULD I DO IT AGAIN?

....

MOMENT THREE

DATE OF MOMENT:

....

....

....

DETAILS OF MOMENT:

....

....

....

HOW IT MADE ME FEEL:

....

....

....

WOULD I DO IT AGAIN?

....

....

MOMENT FOUR

DATE OF MOMENT: ....
....
....

DETAILS OF MOMENT: ....
....
....

HOW IT MADE ME FEEL: ....
....
....

WOULD I DO IT AGAIN? ....

....

MOMENT FIVE

DATE OF MOMENT:
....
....
....

DETAILS OF MOMENT:
....
....
....

HOW IT MADE ME FEEL:
....
....
....

WOULD I DO IT AGAIN?
....
....

April

MOMENT ONE

DATE OF MOMENT:
....

....

DETAILS OF MOMENT:
....

....

....

HOW IT MADE ME FEEL:
....

....

....

WOULD I DO IT AGAIN?
....

....

MOMENT TWO

DATE OF MOMENT:

....

....

....

DETAILS OF MOMENT:

....

....

....

HOW IT MADE ME FEEL:

....

....

....

WOULD I DO IT AGAIN?

....

....

MOMENT THREE

DATE OF MOMENT:
....
....
....

DETAILS OF MOMENT:
....
....
....

HOW IT MADE ME FEEL:
....
....
....

WOULD I DO IT AGAIN?
....
....

MOMENT FOUR

DATE OF MOMENT:

....

....

DETAILS OF MOMENT:

....

....

HOW IT MADE ME FEEL:

....

....

WOULD I DO IT AGAIN?

....

MOMENT FIVE

DATE OF MOMENT:

....

....

DETAILS OF MOMENT:

....

....

HOW IT MADE ME FEEL:

....

....

WOULD I DO IT AGAIN?

....

May

MOMENT ONE

DATE OF MOMENT:

....

....

....

DETAILS OF MOMENT:

....

....

....

HOW IT MADE ME FEEL:

....

....

....

WOULD I DO IT AGAIN?

....

....

MOMENT TWO

DATE OF MOMENT:
....
....
....

DETAILS OF MOMENT:
....
....
....

HOW IT MADE ME FEEL:
....
....
....

WOULD I DO IT AGAIN?
....
....

MOMENT THREE

DATE OF MOMENT:

....

....

....

DETAILS OF MOMENT:

....

....

....

HOW IT MADE ME FEEL:

....

....

....

WOULD I DO IT AGAIN?

....

....

MOMENT FOUR

DATE OF MOMENT:

....

....

DETAILS OF MOMENT:

....

....

HOW IT MADE ME FEEL:

....

....

WOULD I DO IT AGAIN?

....

MOMENT FIVE

DATE OF MOMENT:
....
....
....

DETAILS OF MOMENT:
....
....
....

HOW IT MADE ME FEEL:
....
....
....

WOULD I DO IT AGAIN?
....
....

June

MOMENT ONE

DATE OF MOMENT:
....

....

....

DETAILS OF MOMENT:
....

....

....

HOW IT MADE ME FEEL:
....

....

....

WOULD I DO IT AGAIN?
....

....

MOMENT TWO

DATE OF MOMENT:

....

....

DETAILS OF MOMENT:

....

....

HOW IT MADE ME FEEL:

....

....

WOULD I DO IT AGAIN?

....

MOMENT THREE

DATE OF MOMENT:

....

....

DETAILS OF MOMENT:

....

....

HOW IT MADE ME FEEL:

....

....

WOULD I DO IT AGAIN?

....

MOMENT FOUR

DATE OF MOMENT:

....

....

....

DETAILS OF MOMENT:

....

....

....

HOW IT MADE ME FEEL:

....

....

....

WOULD I DO IT AGAIN?

....

....

MOMENT FIVE

DATE OF MOMENT:

....

....

....

DETAILS OF MOMENT:

....

....

....

HOW IT MADE ME FEEL:

....

....

....

WOULD I DO IT AGAIN?

....

July

MOMENT ONE

DATE OF MOMENT:

....

....

....

DETAILS OF MOMENT:

....

....

....

HOW IT MADE ME FEEL:

....

....

....

WOULD I DO IT AGAIN?

....

....

MOMENT TWO

DATE OF MOMENT:

....

....

DETAILS OF MOMENT:

....

....

HOW IT MADE ME FEEL:

....

....

WOULD I DO IT AGAIN?

....

MOMENT THREE

DATE OF MOMENT:

....

....

....

DETAILS OF MOMENT:

....

....

....

HOW IT MADE ME FEEL:

....

....

....

WOULD I DO IT AGAIN?

....

....

MOMENT FOUR

DATE OF MOMENT:
....
....
....

DETAILS OF MOMENT:
....
....
....

HOW IT MADE ME FEEL:
....
....
....

WOULD I DO IT AGAIN?
....
....

MOMENT FIVE

DATE OF MOMENT:
....

....

....

DETAILS OF MOMENT:
....

....

....

HOW IT MADE ME FEEL:
....

....

....

WOULD I DO IT AGAIN?
....

....

August

MOMENT ONE

DATE OF MOMENT:

....

....

....

DETAILS OF MOMENT:

....

....

....

HOW IT MADE ME FEEL:

....

....

....

WOULD I DO IT AGAIN?

....

MOMENT TWO

DATE OF MOMENT:
....
....
....

DETAILS OF MOMENT:
....
....
....

HOW IT MADE ME FEEL:
....
....
....

WOULD I DO IT AGAIN?
....
....

MOMENT THREE

DATE OF MOMENT:

....

....

....

DETAILS OF MOMENT:

....

....

....

HOW IT MADE ME FEEL:

....

....

....

WOULD I DO IT AGAIN?

....

....

MOMENT FOUR

DATE OF MOMENT:
....
....
....

DETAILS OF MOMENT:
....
....
....

HOW IT MADE ME FEEL:
....
....
....

WOULD I DO IT AGAIN?
....
....

MOMENT FIVE

DATE OF MOMENT:
....
....
....

DETAILS OF MOMENT:
....
....
....

HOW IT MADE ME FEEL:
....
....
....

WOULD I DO IT AGAIN? ....
....

September

MOMENT ONE

DATE OF MOMENT:

....

....

....

DETAILS OF MOMENT:

....

....

....

HOW IT MADE ME FEEL:

....

....

....

WOULD I DO IT AGAIN?

....

....

MOMENT TWO

DATE OF MOMENT:
....
....
....

DETAILS OF MOMENT:
....
....
....

HOW IT MADE ME FEEL:
....
....
....

WOULD I DO IT AGAIN?
....
....

MOMENT THREE

DATE OF MOMENT:
....
....
....

DETAILS OF MOMENT:
....
....
....

HOW IT MADE ME FEEL:
....
....
....

WOULD I DO IT AGAIN?
....
....

MOMENT FOUR

DATE OF MOMENT:
....

....

....

DETAILS OF MOMENT:
....

....

....

HOW IT MADE ME FEEL:
....

....

....

WOULD I DO IT AGAIN?
....

....

MOMENT FIVE

DATE OF MOMENT:

....

....

....

DETAILS OF MOMENT:

....

....

....

HOW IT MADE ME FEEL:

....

....

....

WOULD I DO IT AGAIN?

....

....

October

MOMENT ONE

DATE OF MOMENT:

....

....

DETAILS OF MOMENT:

....

....

HOW IT MADE ME FEEL:

....

....

WOULD I DO IT AGAIN?

....

MOMENT TWO

DATE OF MOMENT:
....
....

DETAILS OF MOMENT:
....
....
....

HOW IT MADE ME FEEL:
....
....

WOULD I DO IT AGAIN?
....
....

MOMENT THREE

DATE OF MOMENT: ....
....
....

DETAILS OF MOMENT: ....
....
....

HOW IT MADE ME FEEL: ....
....
....

WOULD I DO IT AGAIN? ....
....

MOMENT FOUR

DATE OF MOMENT:

....
....
....

DETAILS OF MOMENT:

....
....
....

HOW IT MADE ME FEEL:

....
....
....

WOULD I DO IT AGAIN?

....
....

MOMENT FIVE

DATE OF MOMENT:
....
....
....

DETAILS OF MOMENT:
....
....
....

HOW IT MADE ME FEEL:
....
....
....

WOULD I DO IT AGAIN?
....
....

November

MOMENT ONE

DATE OF MOMENT:
....
....
....

DETAILS OF MOMENT:
....
....
....

HOW IT MADE ME FEEL:
....
....
....

WOULD I DO IT AGAIN?
....
....

MOMENT TWO

DATE OF MOMENT:
....
....
....

DETAILS OF MOMENT:
....
....
....

HOW IT MADE ME FEEL:
....
....
....

WOULD I DO IT AGAIN?
....
....

MOMENT THREE

DATE OF MOMENT:
....
....
....

DETAILS OF MOMENT:
....
....
....

HOW IT MADE ME FEEL:
....
....
....

WOULD I DO IT AGAIN?
....
....

MOMENT FOUR

DATE OF MOMENT:
....

....

....

DETAILS OF MOMENT:
....

....

....

HOW IT MADE ME FEEL:
....

....

....

WOULD I DO IT AGAIN?
....

....

MOMENT FIVE

DATE OF MOMENT:

....

....

....

DETAILS OF MOMENT:

....

....

....

HOW IT MADE ME FEEL:

....

....

....

WOULD I DO IT AGAIN?

....

....

December

MOMENT ONE

DATE OF MOMENT:
....
....
....

DETAILS OF MOMENT:
....
....
....

HOW IT MADE ME FEEL:
....
....
....

WOULD I DO IT AGAIN?
....
....

MOMENT TWO

DATE OF MOMENT:

....

....

....

DETAILS OF MOMENT:

....

....

....

HOW IT MADE ME FEEL:

....

....

....

WOULD I DO IT AGAIN?

....

MOMENT THREE

DATE OF MOMENT:
....

....

....

DETAILS OF MOMENT:
....

....

....

HOW IT MADE ME FEEL:
....

....

....

WOULD I DO IT AGAIN?
....

....

MOMENT FOUR

DATE OF MOMENT:
....
....
....

DETAILS OF MOMENT:
....
....
....

HOW IT MADE ME FEEL:
....
....
....

WOULD I DO IT AGAIN?
....
....

MOMENT FIVE

DATE OF MOMENT:

....

....

....

DETAILS OF MOMENT:

....

....

....

HOW IT MADE ME FEEL:

....

....

....

WOULD I DO IT AGAIN?

....

....

I FELT MY LUNGS INFLATE WITH
THE ONRUSH OF SCENERY
– AIR, MOUNTAINS, TREES,
PEOPLE. I THOUGHT, "THIS IS
WHAT IT IS TO BE HAPPY."

Sylvia Plath

CONCLUSION

Hopefully, by this point, the joy of collecting moments and not things has resonated with you and the ideas have sparked an energy within you that will make you want to get out there and live your best life. Moments are everything in life, and whether they are shared or experienced alone, they will allow you to shape an existence that you are content with. It's time to start collecting those magical moments in the memory bank now!

Image credits

Have you enjoyed this book?
If so, why not write a review
on your favourite website?

If you're interested in finding out more
about our books, find us on Facebook
at **Summersdale Publishers** and follow
us on Twitter at **@Summersdale**.

Thanks very much for buying
this Summersdale book.

www.summersdale.com